MAT MAN

HATS

By Jan Z. Olsen • Illustrations by Molly Delaney

GET SET FOR SCHOOL®

Handwriting Without Tears®
Jan Z. Olsen, OTR

8001 MacArthur Blvd
Cabin John, MD 20818
301.263.2700
www.getsetforschool.com

Printed in Hong Kong

First Edition
ISBN: 978-1-891627-93-4
78910REGAL171615

If we gave Mat Man a hat,
what would Mat Man do?

Turn the page and we'll show you.

With this hard hat

Mat Man is a builder.

I built this treehouse.

I'm very strong.

KIDS ONLY

I saw and hammer all day long.

With this space helmet

Mat Man is an astronaut.

Here I am in outer space.

The earth looks like
a tiny place.

With this batter's helmet

Mat Man is a baseball player.

Batter up!
I swing. I miss. I try one more.

I hit.
I run.
I slide.
I score.

With this helmet

Mat Man is a firefighter.

The fire alarm rings night and day.

Quick! Grab your boots.
We're on the way.

With this cap

Mat Man is a farmer.

I milk the cows and plant the wheat.

I grow the food that you will eat.

With this helmet

Mat Man is a bike racer.

People cheer as I race by.

I pedal so fast. I almost fly.

With this diving helmet

Mat Man is a diver.

I dive down.
The water is clear.

Colorful fish come swimming near.

With this cap

Mat Man is a letter carrier.

Hot or cold, rain or sleet,

I deliver the mail on your street.

With this helmet

Mat Man is a miner.

It's very dark down in the mine.
My helmet shines. I see just fine.

With this hat

Mat Man is a pirate.

I sail for days on the ocean blue.

Looking for treasure is what I do.

With this hat

Mat Man is a cowboy.

I spend my days in the saddle.

My horse and I
are herding cattle.

With this chef's cap

Mat Man is a baker.

What tasty treat would you like to try?

Do you want cake or pie?

With this cap

Mat Man is a pilot.

All the systems check out right.

We're cleared for take-off on this flight.

With this hat

Mat Man is a clown.

My funny bike has a wiggle.

It looks so silly,
it makes you giggle.

With this top hat

Mat Man is a magician.

Abracadabra, zippity zoo!

Here's a bunny just for you.

Mat Man puts on his sleeping cap.

Now it's time to take a nap.